P9-EJH-596

POODLE: The Other White Meat

The Second *Sherman's Lagoon* Collection
by Jim Toomey

WITHDRAWN

Andrews McMeel
Publishing

Kansas City

To Charlie and Sam

Sherman's Lagoon is distributed internationally by King Features Syndicate, Inc. For information, write King Features Syndicate, Inc., 235 East 45th Street, New York, New York 10017.

Poodle: The Other White Meat copyright © 1999 by J.P. Toomey. All rights reserved. Printed in the United States of America. No part of this book may be used or reproduced in any manner whatsoever without written permission except in the case of reprints in the context of reviews. For information, write Andrews McMeel Publishing, an Andrews McMeel Universal company, 4520 Main Street, Kansas City, Missouri 64111.

www.andrewsmcmeel.com

99 00 01 02 03 BAH 10 9 8 7 6 5 4 3 2

ISBN: 0-8362-8287-6

Library of Congress Catalog Card Number: 98-88677

WITHDRAWN

Sherman's Lagoon may be viewed on the world wide web at:
www.slagoon.com

―――― **ATTENTION: SCHOOLS AND BUSINESSES** ――――

Andrews McMeel books are available at quantity discounts with bulk purchase for educational, business, or sales promotional use. For information, please write to: Special Sales Department, Andrews McMeel Publishing, 4520 Main Street, Kansas City, Missouri 64111.

Introduction

I love poodles. And not broiled on a skewer. I prefer them alive and unclipped—the way they were before humans tamed them. When I was a boy, my family had a toy poodle named Sam. My parents purchased Sam with the intention of diversifying the family dog portfolio, which at the time consisted of a golden retriever. Coiffed and well schooled, Sam was supposed to be the cultured counterpart to the Golden Slobbering Mammal. Sam went his own way, however. He dropped out of obedience school and grew his hair long. He came to resemble a pygmy woolly mammoth with dreadlocks. He would lumber into the house wearing a menagerie of leaves, gumballs, and dead bugs like a self-propelled dust mop. Oh sure, Sam would get his annual clip, and for a few weeks he'd look like a shrub from Versailles, but despite his poodle exterior he was still Sam.

Sam is a good case study in animal behavior. You might suppose that when Sam metamorphosed annually from woolly mammoth to Versailles shrub, his attitude would change as well, but it wasn't the case. This observation leads me to a radical theory that animals are completely unaware of their exterior. I've noticed that dogs generally walk right past mirrors and don't stop to tidy up their coat. Charlie, the aforementioned golden retriever, once walked around all day with an extra eye on her forehead that I had drawn in her fur with a Magic Marker. It didn't seem to phase her. What's more amazing is, if the other dogs noticed, they weren't letting on. Which leads me to an even more radical theory that I'll call the Universal Theory of Animal Self and Mutual Cosmetic Unawareness. Basically, animals don't care what they look like nor what their friends look like.

So why should we? Some animals are lucky enough to be "cute" in our eyes and therefore we hairless beach apes tend to feel more empathy toward them. Philosophers have been trying to quantify cute for centuries. Plato might say that there's an ultimate cute form, something resembling a Teletubby, by which we measure earthbound cute things. Dolphins for example are cute. Their eyes have a knowing look to them. Their mouths are upturned into a permanent smile. And most of all, dolphins are "intelligent" and trainable. That is, we can alter their software and get them to do cute things that wild dolphins wouldn't be caught dead doing. A shark on the other hand is farther from the Teletubby ideal. A shark has "lifeless eyes, like a doll's eyes," as Quint from *Jaws* would say. And the system software in a shark, some of the most elegant code ever written by Mother Nature, code that took 300 million years to perfect, is basically read-only. That is, you'll never get a shark to waddle out of the water and balance a china plate on its nose. The fact that many species of sharks are teetering on the brink of extinction is a well-kept secret. Which leads me to yet another radical theory called the Law of Hairless Beach Ape Empathy toward Teletubby-Like Creatures. In other words, we humans care about the cute animals, but the "ugly" ones will have to figure out a way to save themselves.

All this is a long-winded introduction to what I really wanted to say in this introduction. That is, to answer a question I hear all the time: Why a comic strip about fish? If the above Theory of Empathy holds true, fish are the least likely candidates to populate a successful comic strip. Well, call me a contrarian, or call me a fool. But, while "cute" is hopelessly anchored to the Teletubby ideal, "ugly" is free to take infinite varieties. In this way, ugly is beautiful, to a cartoonist at least. And so, I've taken some of the "ugly" animals and tried to think like them and talk like them, and I've come up with some interesting results. By way of this book, I hope to inspire my readers to look at a flounder and see not an ugly flat fish, but a living, breathing thing with hobbies, interests, relationship problems, and possibly a rotating credit card debt just like you and me.

GROSS. WHAT'S ALL THIS GUNK IN THE WATER?

FISH GUTS.

SOME GIANT TUNA TRAWLER JUST DUMPED IT RIGHT ON TOP OF ME.

THIS IS WHAT I ALWAYS IMAGINED **HEAVEN** TO BE LIKE.

WHAT RELIGION ARE **YOU**?

FOR MY HOMEWORK I'M SUPPOSED TO INTERVIEW ALL THE ANIMALS IN THE LAGOON... ARE YOU REALLY A GREAT WHITE SHARK?

(MUNCH) I GUESS SO.

YOU'RE NOT GREAT, AND YOU'RE NOT WHITE - YOU'RE GRAY. I'LL PUT DOWN "GRAY SHARK."

I AM TOO GREAT! PUT DOWN "GREAT GRAY SHARK"!

I'VE GOT A BETTER NAME. "BIG JUNK FOOD-EATING BLOB."

GREAT BIG JUNK FOOD-EATING BLOB.

OKAY, WE'LL COMPROMISE.

I'M INTERVIEWING ALL OF THE ANIMALS IN THE LAGOON... YOU'RE A GREEN SEA TURTLE, CORRECT?

OUTSIDE I'M GREEN, BUT INSIDE I'M A BLUE SEA TURTLE...

...DESPERATELY SEEKING A NEW SHE-TURTLE... SOMEONE TO CALL MY SWEET PEA TURTLE.

ANY HOBBIES BESIDES BAD POETRY?

I'M A BAD COOK.

5

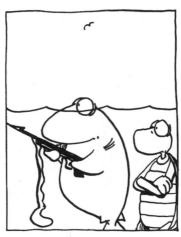

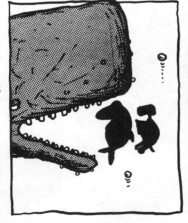

THE NAVY SEALS HAVE RETREATED FROM THE LAGOON! VICTORY IS OURS!

YOUR SILLY CRAB ARMY HAD NOTHING TO DO WITH IT. THEY LEFT BECAUSE THEY FINISHED THEIR WAR GAMES.

HUMBUG! IT WAS A BRILLIANT MILITARY STRATEGY TIMED PERFECTLY.

YEAH, SURE.

WE'RE OFF TO GO KICK THE BRITISH OUT OF HONG KONG.

TOO LATE.

WHOA NELLY, WATER LEVEL'S LOOKING A LITTLE LOW.

IT IS?

MUST BE A LEAK IN THE LAGOON.

REALLY?

OH WELL, IT'S ALL THE SAME TO US CRABS. WE GO BOTH WAYS.

C'MON, A LITTLE FRESH AIR'S GOOD FOR YOU.

COUGH!

THE WATER LEVEL IS DOWN ANOTHER 4 INCHES TODAY...

THE MONSOONS ARE LATE THIS YEAR. WE'LL ALL HAVE TO ADJUST TO USING LESS WATER TILL THE RAINS COME.

SOME OF US SEEM TO BE ADJUSTING BETTER THAN OTHERS.

DELIVERY FOR A MS. IDA VAN BUREN.

OH GOOD... THE AIRLINE FOUND MY LUGGAGE. WHAT TOOK SO LONG?

IT FELL OUT OF YOUR AIRPLANE IN MID-FLIGHT AND WAS EVENTUALLY RECOVERED BY A FISHERMAN ON THE REMOTE ISLAND OF KAPUPU.

YOU CAN SEE WHERE SOME SHARK CHEWED ON THE HANDLE.

HEH HEH... WELL, YOUNG MAN, YOU CERTAINLY HAVE A VIVID IMAGINATION.

HEEEEERE'S JOHNNY...

HAWTHORNE! WHERE IN THE BLAZES **ARE** YOU?

I'VE SMUGGLED MYSELF INTO THE HOME OF SOME HAIRLESS BEACH APE.

WHY?

MILES FROM THE NEAREST OCEAN, I'M PERFECTLY POSITIONED TO MOUNT A SURGICAL STRIKE AGAINST THEIR INFRASTRUCTURE.

UH OH... TROUBLE... SHE'S GOT HOSTAGES.

FILLMORE, THIS IS HAWTHORNE REPORTING IN FROM THE HOME OF MS. IDA VAN BUREN... I'VE SOLVED THE HOSTAGE CRISIS... OVER.

YOU RESCUED HER TROPICAL FISH?

AFFIRMATIVE. THEY'RE ON THEIR WAY BACK TO THE OCEAN VIA A COMPLEX UNDERGROUND NETWORK.

YOU DIDN'T FLUSH THEM DOWN THE TOILET, DID YOU?

IS THAT A PROBLEM?

SHERMAN'S LAGOON

BY o'TOMEY

SHERMAN! WATCH OUT FOR THAT...

...SPEEDBOAT.

VROOM!

THERE MUST BE A GLITCH IN THE NEW COMPUTER... YOU'VE BEEN SENT TO HOG'S HEAVEN.

WORKS FOR ME.

MUNCH MUNCH OINK! MUNCH

SHARK HEAVEN'S ON CLOUD 48... REGISTRATION'S ON THE THIRD FLOOR.

TAP TAP TAP TAP

POOF!

THEY SENT YOU **HERE**?

THIS ISN'T SHARK HEAVEN?

NO. AND I DON'T HAVE TIME TO DEAL WITH THIS RIGHT NOW...

AOOOOOOOOOH!

...I'M JUST GOING TO DELETE YOUR FILE.

TAP TAP TAP

POOF!

DOGS, HUH?

YEP... AND IF IT WEREN'T FOR THAT NEW COMPUTER SYTSTEM, I'D BE A GONER.

HEAD INJURY.

HAWTHORNE, IT'S DANGEROUS FOR A HERMIT CRAB TO BE WANDERING AROUND IN SOMEBODY'S HOUSE.

IT'S OKAY... SHE WENT TO WORK... I HAVE THE PLACE TO MYSELF... I'M GOING TO POKE AROUND.

UH OH... FILLMORE, I THINK THIS WOMAN'S A SERIAL KILLER...

I FOUND A BUNCH OF HEADLESS SHRIMP IN THE FREEZER.

GET OUT OF THERE RIGHT AWAY!

I'M AFRAID WE MIGHT'VE SEEN THE LAST OF OUR BUDDY HAWTHORNE.

A HERMIT CRAB STRANDED THOUSANDS OF MILES INLAND... HOW'S HE EVER GOING TO GET BACK?

VROOOOM!

SPLASH!

IT'S MARKED "DANGEROUS GOODS."

HE FED EXED HIMSELF.

I BROUGHT SOME BROCHURES HOME TO HELP US PLAN OUR EUROPEAN VACATION, SHERMAN.

THE FJORDS OF NORWAY ARE POPULAR WITH SHARKS THIS YEAR.

NAH...

HOW 'BOUT THE FRENCH RIVIERA?

NAH...

THE CANALS OF VENICE?

HAVEN'T EATEN ITALIAN AWHILE.

SO THIS IS VENICE.

ISN'T IT BEAUTIFUL, SHERMAN?

WHAT DOES "THE SHARK'S GUIDE TO VENICE" SAY ABOUT THIS PLACE?

RIGHT NOW WE'RE SWIMMING UNDER THE BRIDGE OF SANTA LUCIA DELLA MARCO, BUILT IN 1427...

...EVERY SUNDAY AT 4 O'CLOCK THEY THROW A SOCCER REFEREE OFF THIS BRIDGE.

I THINK I'M GOING TO LIKE ITALY.

ISN'T IT ROMANTIC, SHERMAN? HERE WE ARE IN A CANAL IN VENICE, SITTING AT A CAFÉ, WATCHING THE GONDOLAS GO BY.

FOOD'S HERE!

WHAT DID YOU ORDER?

CLOMP!

VENETIAN-ON-A-STICK.

HOW'RE YOU SUPPOSED TO EAT IT?

I'VE GOT AN IDEA, MEGAN. LET'S TRY TO GET FRIENDLY WITH ONE OF THE LOCALS. WHAT'S ITALIAN FOR "HELLO"?

CIAO.

CIAO.

VATTENE, STUPIDO.

ITALIAN IS SUCH A BEAUTIFUL LANGUAGE.

HE JUST CALLED YOU A MORON.

SHERMAN'S LAGOON

BY J.P. TOOMEY

IT'S CAPT. QUIGLEY AGAIN... BOY, HE NEVER GIVES UP.

TAP TAP TAP TAP

WELCOME TO STRATEGIC COMMAND NETLINK

BUY SHARK REPELLENT

LET'S SEE... USER NAME... BILL CLINTON. HMM... I'LL BET HIS PASSWORD IS "BIG MAC"... BINGO!

TAP TAP TAP

IT'S THE PRESIDENT, GENERAL. HE'S ORDERED A STRIKE IN QUADRANT 45G... 12 DEGREES SOUTH LATITUDE, 178 DEGREES WEST LONGITUDE.

PLOP!

PLOP!

NICE SHOT.

I'LL HAVE TO BOOKMARK THAT WEBSITE.

24

SHERMAN'S LAGOON

BY J. TOOMEY

SHERMAN'S LAGOON

BY J.P. TOOMEY

I CAN'T HEAR ANYTHING.

LET ME TRY.

HMPH... ME NEITHER.

YOUR EARS ARE AS BAD AS MINE.

HUH?

HOW'S THE DIET?

SWALLOWED AN ANCHOR A COUPLE OF WEEKS AGO.

WELL, AN ANCHOR OR TWO WON'T DO ANY HARM.

I DIDN'T THINK SO.

YOU'RE HEALTHY AS A HORSE. SEE YOU NEXT YEAR.

OKEY DOKEY.

WHY DON'T YOU GET A SECOND OPINION FROM A DOCTOR WHO **ISN'T** EXACTLY LIKE YOU?

I TRUST THIS GUY.

SHERMAN'S LAGOON

BY J.P. TOOMEY

JUST YESTERDAY I WAS A FISH AND YOU WERE A SEA TURTLE. NOW LOOK AT US.

TWO HUMANS SITTING IN CAPTAIN QUIGLEY'S SEAFOOD RESTAURANT.

LOOK AT THOSE POOR LOBSTERS. THIS PLACE GIVES ME THE CREEPS.

WE HAVE TO REMEMBER WHY WE'RE HERE... TO RESCUE HAWTHORNE.

OKAY, WHAT'LL IT BE FOR DINNER?

HAWTHORNE? IS THAT YOU?

YOU'RE A WAITER HERE?

ACTUALLY, I'M THE COOK.

A CRAB!.. ONE OF OUR VERY OWN... A FELLOW SEA CREATURE... WORKING IN A SEAFOOD RESTAURANT!

SHAME ON YOU.

CATCH O' THE DAY: FLOUNDER

IT'S JUST A STEPPING STONE TO A BIGGER CAREER IN THE SEAFOOD INDUSTRY.

CATCH THE DAY FLOUND

YOU CONNIVING LITTLE BUG! YOU'D DO ANYTHING FOR POWER, EVEN IF IT MEANS MURDERING YOUR FELLOW SEA CREATURES!

CATCH O' THE DAY FLOUNDER

YOU'D MAKE A GOOD DICTATOR!

YOU'D MAKE A GOOD GUMBO!

LET ME OUT OF THIS BOX!

WE'RE TAKING YOU BACK TO THE LAGOON. IT'S FOR YOUR OWN GOOD.

A CRAB HAS NO BUSINESS WORKING IN A SEAFOOD RESTAURANT.

NOW LET US TAKE OUR LEAVE OF THIS DISGUSTING PLACE AND RETURN TO OUR PEACEFUL COEXISTENCE AS SEA CREATURES.

SEAFO

ONE BROILED SALMON TO GO.

THAT'S ME.

SHERMAN'S LAGOON

BY J. TOOMEY

Sherman's Lagoon

BY J TOOMEY

SHARK FOOD
CONTENTS: HAIRLESS BEACH APE, SURFBOARD, SUNBLOCK.

WHATCHA WORKIN' ON, FAT BOY?

TRYIN' TO OPEN THIS CAN I FOUND. I THINK THERE'S SOMETHING TO EAT INSIDE.

YOU WOULDN'T HAVE ANYTHING IN THAT DRAB LITTLE CRAB HOLE THAT RESEMBLES A CAN OPENER, WOULD YOU?

HERE'S A SHARP ROCK.

THAT'LL HAVE TO DO, I GUESS.

WELL, WOULDJA LOOK AT THAT! IT'S A BABY SEA TURTLE!

ISN'T HE CUTE?

FOUND HIM ON ASCENSION ISLAND, SO I ADOPTED HIM.

HE LOOKS JUST LIKE YOU 'CEPT HE'S A TENTH THE SIZE.

AND ONLY A TENTH THE CALORIES.

TOUCH HIM, YOU'RE DEAD.

WANNA HOLD MY BABY SEA TURTLE, MEGAN?

SURE. WHAT'S HIS NAME?

I HAVEN'T NAMED HIM YET.

YOU REALLY OUGHTA GIVE THE LITTLE GUY A NAME.

ANY CHILD OF MINE NEES A DIGNIFIED NAME...

A NAME WITH WHICH HE CAN RUN FOR PRESIDENT.

HOW ABOUT "LITTLE POOPER"?

ERNEST, I'D LIKE YOU TO MEET MY NEW ADOPTED SON, CLAYTON.

HELLO CLAYTON.

300 MEGAHERTZ MICROPROCESSOR.

HIS FIRST WORDS! CLAYTON JUST SPOKE HIS FIRST WORDS!

HE'S ONLY A FEW WEEKS OLD AND HE ALREADY KNOWS MORE ABOUT COMPUTERS THAN ME.

GET USED TO IT.

Panel 1: LOOK, ERNEST, IT'S A SEA CAVE! / IT'S NOT JUST A CAVE, IT'S AN OPPORTUNITY.

Panel 2: AN OPPORTUNITY? / YEAH... TO EXPLORE NEW TERRITORY, CONFRONT NEW DANGERS, LEARN NEW THINGS ABOUT THE WORLD AROUND US.

Panel 3: WHAT WOULD YOU DO IN THE FACE OF SUCH AN OPPORTUNITY?

Panel 4: EAT SOME PIE. / NO! CHARGE IN!

Panel 5: COOL! LOOK AT THESE CAVE PAINTINGS, SHERMAN. / WHOA NELLY. WONDER HOW OLD THEY ARE.

Panel 6: PRETTY OLD... LOOK, THERE'S A PICTURE OF A PLESIOSAUR.

Panel 7: WELL, THAT'S INTERESTING... SHARKS HAD LEGS BACK THEN. / REALLY?

Panel 8: AND A LARGER SKULL. / I'M NOT EVOLVING, I'M DE-VOLVING.

Panel 9: HEY SHERM, DO YOU REMEMBER HOW TO GET OUT OF THIS CAVE? / FEAR NOT, ERNEST. SHARKS HAVE AN ACUTE SENSE OF SMELL. I'LL SNIFF OUR WAY OUT.

Panel 10: (SNIFF) HMPH... WELL, THERE'S GOOD NEWS AND BAD NEWS.

Panel 11: GIMME THE BAD NEWS FIRST. / I CAN'T SMELL FILLMORE'S AFTERSHAVE ANYMORE. THAT MEANS WE'RE FAR FROM HOME.

Panel 12: WHAT'S THE GOOD NEWS? / I CAN'T SMELL FILLMORE'S AFTERSHAVE ANYMORE.

SHERMAN'S LAGOON

BY J TOOMEY

WHAT DO YOU WANT ON YOUR PIZZA... PEPPERONI OR SAUSAGE?

THAT'S JUST THE KIND OF MULTIVARIABLE PROBLEM THAT'S PERFECT FOR A COMPUTER SPREADSHEET.

OH NO... NOT ANOTHER SPREAD-SHEET.

LET'S QUANTIFY OUR PARAMETERS... ON A SCALE FROM 1 TO 10 RATE YOUR INGREDIENTS.

PEPPERONI 8, SAUSAGE 3.

I'LL GIVE SAUSAGE A 7, PEPPERONI A 4... NOW LET'S DIVIDE BY OUR RESPECTIVE WEIGHTS... DO A LITTLE FORMATTING.

TAP TAP TAP

PRESTO, THE ANSWER IS 48.

48? WHAT'S THAT SUPPOSED TO MEAN?

IT MEANS 48. YOU CAN'T ARGUE WITH A NUMBER, FILLMORE.

BUT HOW DOES THIS RESULT GET US ANY CLOSER TO A DECISION?

LET'S FLIP A COIN.

HEADS WE GET PEPPERONI.

SHERMAN'S LAGOON

BY TOOMEY

STOP PINCHING TOES IN 30 DAYS THROUGH HYPNOSIS

HAVE YOU KICKED THAT NASTY TOE PINCHING HABIT, HAWTHORNE?

I'M IN MY FOURTH WEEK... THIS IS THE TURNING POINT.

BUT THE DOCTOR SAYS I CAN PINCH ONE TOE PER DAY, AND—GUESS WHAT, MR. TOE?— YOU'RE OUR LUCKY WINNER.

WHAT? NO SCREAM?

WHAT A RIP-OFF! I TAKE MY ONE-AND-ONLY DAILY TOE PINCH, AND I DIDN'T EVEN GET A SCREAM!

ARGH!

OUCH!

THERE HE GOES AGAIN.

DOWN THE SLIPPERY SLOPE.

OW! OOH!

SHERMAN'S LAGOON

BY J.P. TOOMEY

SHERMAN, LOOK AT MY FIN! IT'S DROOPING!

IT HAPPENS TO ALL SHARKS WHEN THEY HIT THAT CERTAIN AGE, MEGAN.

WELL, I WASN'T AWARE THAT I WAS EVEN REMOTELY CLOSE TO THAT CERTAIN AGE, THANK YOU VERY MUCH.

I'M GETTING OLD! MY BODY IS FALLING APART! YESTERDAY MY FIN WAS FINE, TODAY IT'S DROOPING!

TOMORROW I'LL BE A CAN OF CAT FOOD!

YOU'RE SKIPPING A FEW DAYS IN THERE.

ARGH! SHARK!

WAIT A MINUTE...

NOT TO WORRY. IT'S GOT A DROOPY FIN. IT'S JUST SOME DROOPY-FINNED OVER-THE-HILL SHARK.

BOY, THEY SURE KNOW HOW TO PUSH YOUR BUTTONS.

I'M NOT EVEN HUNGRY, BUT I GUESS I CAN FORCE SOMETHING DOWN.

SAYS RIGHT HERE IN "MARTHA STEWART'S LIVING WITH FIN DROOP" THAT A DROOPY FIN IS CAUSED BY A VITAMIN B DEFICIENCY.

THAT'S IT! I NEED MORE VITAMIN B!

CRABS CONTAIN VITAMIN B.

WHICH WAY DID SHE GO?

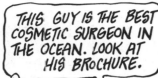

YOU WANT TO GET A FIN LIFT?

SURGERY IS THE ONLY WAY TO CORRECT FIN DROOP, SHERMAN.

THIS GUY IS THE BEST COSMETIC SURGEON IN THE OCEAN. LOOK AT HIS BROCHURE.

WOW.

THAT FLOUNDER USED TO HAVE BOTH EYES ON ONE SIDE OF HIS FACE... NOW LOOK AT HIM.

HE LOOKS JUST LIKE ELVIS.

NOT BAD, HUH?

WELL, THE COSMETIC SURGERY WAS A SUCCESS, I GUESS.

MY FIN ISN'T DROOPING ANYMORE.

NOPE. EVERYTHING LOOKS TIGHT AS A DRUM.

I WOULD WHOLEHEARTEDLY RECOMMEND A FIN LIFT TO ANY OF MY FRIENDS.

DIDN'T YOU USED TO HAVE GILLS?

THEY'RE ON THE BACK OF MY HEAD NOW.

SHERMAN, LOOK AT ME! MY COSMETIC SURGERY ONLY LASTED A DAY! THAT DOCTOR IS A COMPLETE QUACK! LET'S LITIGATE!

ALLOW ME TO INTRODUCE MYSELF... ELSWORTH HAGFISH III, ATTORNEY-AT-LAW.

ARGH!

GULP!

IT'S TRUE... THERE'S A LAWYER UNDER EVERY ROCK.

LET'S TRY THIS ROCK.

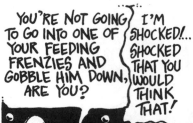

WHY ARE YOU LEAVING A TRAIL OF GREEN M&M'S?

I'M HOPING TO ATTRACT OUR BABY SEA TURTLE.

MAKES SENSE... TURTLES ARE GREEN – THEY PROBABLY LIKE GREEN M&M'S.

I FORGOT... SO DO KILLER WHALES.

GIVE HIM THE WHOLE BAG.

YOU FOUND HIM!

SOME BABYSITTER YOU ARE! YOU CAN'T EVEN TAKE CARE OF ONE BABY SEA TURTLE!

I'M SORRY I LOST HIM, MEGAN.

WHAT IF SOME BABYSITTER LOST ONE OF **OUR** KIDS? HOW WOULD YOU FEEL?

PRETTY DARNED ROTTEN.

HMPH!

HOW WOULD **YOU** FEEL?

NO PROBLEMO. HERMIT CRABS COME IN LITTERS OF 2000.

FILLMORE, YOU'RE BACK SO SOON! I WAS JUST GETTING THE HANG OF THIS BABYSITTING THING.

HOW'S CLAYTON?

HE'S DOING FINE. WATCH HOW EASILY I CAN GET HIM TO GO TO SLEEP.

JUST GIVE HIM A GOOD SPIN, AND HE PASSES RIGHT OUT.

I'LL TAKE HIM NOW.

MEGAN, WHY DID YOU THROW AWAY MY BOX OF SUPER SUGAR SMACKS?

IT WAS EMPTY.

I HAVEN'T FINISHED READING IT YET.

HELLO.

ARGH! A HEADLESS FISH! ... I MEAN A FISHLESS HEAD!

YES, IT'S TRUE... SOME FISHERMAN CUT MY HEAD OFF AND KEPT THE REST OF ME, BUT I LIVED ON!

AND **NOW** I AM DOOMED TO CRAWL ALONG THE OCEAN BOTTOM AS A WARNING TO ALL!

WHAT'S YOUR BETTER HALF UP TO?

GOT ME.

IT'S A TALKING FISH HEAD.

HERE, TAKE HIM.

SOME FISHERMAN CUT MY HEAD OFF, BUT **I LIVED ON!**

I'VE HEARD ALL THIS BEFORE

...AND NOW I AM DOOMED TO CRAWL THE OCEAN BOTTOM AS A WARNING TO ALL! THE STORY I'M ABOUT TO TELL IS NOT FOR THE FAINT OF HEART...

IT'S A TALKING FISH HEAD.

HERE, TAKE HIM.

THAT'S HIM! THAT'S THE FISHERMAN WHO CUT MY HEAD OFF AND KEPT MY BODY.

WE CAN GET THE BODY BACK. THIS IS A JOB FOR COMMANDO CRAB!

GOT IT. NOW LET'S ATTEMPT SURGICAL REATTACHMENT.

THAT'S A SALAMI.

THANKS TO THE MIRACLE OF MODERN MEDICINE, WE HAVE SUCCESSFULLY JOINED A LIVING FISH HEAD TO A SALAMI.

AND NOW THE PATIENT WILL BE ABLE TO LIVE AN ALMOST-NORMAL LIFE AS A SALAMI FISH.

HE'S COMING TO.

THIS IS THE NEW YOU... HAVE A LOOK.

MAYBE TAKE A LITTLE BIT OFF THE BACK.

I'VE GOT A SWISS ARMY KNIFE.

LIFE HAS RETURNED TO NORMAL SINCE MY HEAD WAS SURGICALLY JOINED TO A SALAMI.

THE PRESS HAS STOPPED CALLING... I'M NO LONGER A FREAK IN THE MEDIA LIMELIGHT.

I'M JUST AN ORDINARY SALAMI FISH.

I WISH I WERE AN OSCAR MEYER WIENER FISH.

SAW THAT ONE COMING.

SHERMAN'S LAGOON

BY J. TOOMEY

ERNEST, I THOUGHT YOU INVITED ME ALONG TO SEE "TITANIC" WITH YOU?

I DID.

WELL, HOW MUCH FARTHER IS IT?

LET'S SEE...

WE SHOULD BE IN THE NORTH ATLANTIC BY TOMORROW.

WERE WE TALKING THE SHIP OR THE MOVIE?

THE NORTH ATLANTIC IS GIANT SQUID TERRITORY, ERNEST, SO LET'S KEEP OUR EYES PEELED.

THERE'S ONE!

NOPE. THAT'S A MEDIUM SQUID.

THERE ARE SMALL SQUIDS, MEDIUM SQUIDS, AND GIANT SQUIDS.

YOU ONLY GET 8 SLICES OUT OF A MEDIUM SQUID.

HOW HUNGRY ARE YOU?

COOL! AN UNDERWATER MOUNTAIN RANGE!

THIS PART OF THE OCEAN IS KNOWN AS THE MID-ATLANTIC RIDGE.

I'VE SEEN THIS IN BROCHURES.

NICE VIEW FROM UP HERE.

THIS IS THE PRICIEST REAL ESTATE IN THE OCEAN.

SHOULD'VE BOUGHT WHEN IT WAS CHEAP.

EXCUSE ME, SIR, WOULD THIS SHIPWRECK BE THE FAMOUS TITANIC?

YEP. IT'S #4 TO GET IN.

FOUR BUCKS!

WE'RE APPALLED THAT YOU WOULD TURN THIS HISTORIC AND TRAGIC SHIPWRECK INTO A COMMERCIAL ENTERPRISE!

IT'S STILL FOUR BUCKS.

OKAY, OKAY. WE'VE COME ALL THIS WAY.

HERE ARE YOUR PUTTERS.

IT'S A MINIATURE GOLF COURSE?

THERE MUST BE A NICE PLACE TO RELAX SOMEWHERE ON THIS OLD SUNKEN SHIP.

THERE'S A PLACE.

I PREFER THE VIEW AT THE BACK OF THE SHIP.

ME TOO. LET'S TAKE OUR CHAIRS BACK THERE.

YOU REALIZE WE'RE REARRANGING DECK CHAIRS ON THE TITANIC.

THAT OCCURRED TO ME.

WHAT'S THAT, SHERM?

JUST SOME OLD RELIC I FOUND ON THE TITANIC.

WE SHOULD PROBABLY LEAVE THIS PLACE UNDISTURBED, SHERM.

EVEN THOUGH WE'RE ANIMALS, WE STILL HAVE RESPECT FOR HUMAN TRAGEDY.

FAREWELL, TITANIC. MAY YOU REST IN PEACE.

GOT IT.

SHERMAN'S LAGOON

BY JTOMEY

 CHECK OUT MY NEW TRANSPORTATION. THE CRABSTER, BY CRAB MOTOR WORKS.

 THE NEW C.M.W... WOW, THE STOCK MARKET HAS BEEN GOOD TO YOU.

 YOU THINK RED IS TOO FLASHY? ATTRACTS KILLER WHALES.

 AWWW THIS THING'LL OUTRUN ONE OF THOSE BAGS OF BLUBBER ANY DAY... LATER, POOR BOY.

 ZIP!

 ARGH!

 POOF!

 CLOMP!

 TOTALED IT THE FIRST DAY. LUCKY YOU HAD AIR BAGS.

ARGH! RELAX, I WON'T HARM YOU. I'M A NICE KILLER WHALE. WHERE CAN I HIDE?

HEY, AREN'T YOU THE KILLER WHALE WHO MADE THAT DARING ESCAPE IN "FREE WILLY"?

AND "FREE WILLY PART TWO," **AND** "RETURN OF WILLY"...

...BUT I'M STILL NOT FREE.

THEY'RE STILL AFTER YOU, HUH?

THEY WANT TO DO ANOTHER SEQUEL.

THEY'RE GONE... YOU CAN COME OUT NOW.

I'M FREE! I FINALLY ESCAPED FROM OCEANWORLD AMUSEMENT PARK!

I'VE SPENT THE LAST 15 YEARS OF MY LIFE AS A PERFORMING WHALE, AND NOW I'M ON MY OWN.

THEY SAY LIFE ON THE OUTSIDE CAN BE DIFFICULT.

FIRST THING WE DO IS GET YOU SOME NEW CLOTHES.

FILLMORE, IS IT TRUE THERE'S A **KILLER WHALE** IN THE LAGOON?

YEP.

IS THIS KILLER WHALE AWARE THAT YOURS TRULY IS EL SUPREMO-BADFISH-PREDATOR AROUND HERE, AND I DON'T LOOK KINDLY ON INTRUDERS?

I DON'T BELIEVE HE IS, EL SUPREMO.

GO TELL HIM.

YOU TELL HIM.

I'M NOT GOING NEAR HIM.

Row 1

I GUESS THEY FED YOU PRETTY WELL WHEN YOU WERE A PERFORMER AT OCEANWORLD.

THREE SQUARES A DAY.

YOU'RE ON THE OUTSIDE NOW...UNTIL YOU LEARN HOW TO HUNT FOR YOURSELF, I'LL MAKE SURE YOU DON'T GO HUNGRY.

I'VE NEVER EATEN OFF A PLATE BEFORE.

HOW'S THIS?

MAKE ME JUMP FOR IT.

Row 2

I'M SUPPOSED TO SHOW YOU HOW TO BE A PREDATOR.

GOOD LUCK. I'VE SPENT THE LAST 15 YEARS OF MY LIFE IN A THEME PARK.

I'M NOT A PREDATOR, I'M A PERFORMER. I DO BACK FLIPS. PEOPLE APPLAUD.

THAT'S NICE... IT MUST BE GRATIFYING TO PUT A SMILE ON ALL THOSE PEOPLE'S FACES.

THE PEOPLE CONTACT WAS MY FAVORITE PART OF THE JOB.

PEOPLE HAVE THREE EDIBLE PARTS... LOINS, LEGS, AND RIBS.

SHOULD I TAKE NOTES?

Row 3

THAT WAS MY AGENT ON THE PHONE. I GOT AN OFFER TO DO ANOTHER FREE WILLY MOVIE.

DON'T DO IT!

HE SAYS THIS MOVIE'S GOING TO BE PURE ART... AN OSCAR CONTENDER.

HOLLYWOOD DOESN'T CREATE ART! HOLLYWOOD IS AN EVIL, ICKY, CORRUPT, VILE CESS POOL!

I'M GETTING 10 MILLION BUCKS.

DO THEY NEED A TURTLE?

THEY'RE PUTTING JIM CARREY IN A TURTLE SUIT.

SHERMAN'S LAGOON

BY O'TOOLE(?)

I HAVE YOU IN MY PALM PILOT FOR SUNDAY MORNING... I'M HERE. WHAT'S THE FUN PLAN, FAT BOY?

THE FUN PLAN?

YOU INVITED ME OVER. I'M HERE TO HAVE FUN, AND I DON'T HAVE ALL DAY!

I DON'T HAVE A FUN PLAN.

MY PRECIOUS WEEKEND IS FLEETING BY, AND **YOU** DON'T HAVE A **FUN PLAN?**

LET'S PLAY A GAME.

WHAT KIND OF GAME? THIS BETTER BE A GOOD GAME!

I DON'T KNOW... CARDS, OR SOMETHING.

HRMPH! CARDS?

I KNOW! LET'S PLAY "PINCH THE FAT SHARK!

ARGH!

OWOOOO!

OKAY, THAT WAS FUN. WHAT ARE WE DOING NEXT WEEKEND?

I'M BUSY.

64

SHERMAN, I FEEL IT'S MY OBLIGATION AS A FELLOW SHARK TO INFORM YOU THERE'S A SKIN DIVER IN THE LAGOON.

OF COURSE IT'S OF NO INTEREST TO ME, SINCE I'VE RECENTLY BECOME A VEGETARIAN.

NOPE, I'LL HAVE NONE OF THAT. I'M A PEACE-LOVING NON-MEATEATING SOUL.

WHERE IS HE?

RIGHT HERE.

HEY MEGAN, I THOUGHT YOU BECAME A VEGETARIAN?

I DIDN'T TOTALLY GO OFF THE DEEP END... I STILL EAT DAIRY PRODUCTS.

THAT'S A 3 INCH THICK PORTERHOUSE STEAK.

COWS ARE DAIRY PRODUCTS.

TECHNICALLY YES.

LUNCHTIME... MY FAVORITE TIME OF DAY.

NEXT TO DINNER TIME.

WITH BREAKFAST TIME RUNNING A CLOSE THIRD.

CLICK

UH OH... SHE DID IT TO ME AGAIN.

A TUNA FISH.

THIRD TIME THIS WEEK.

WATCH THIS BARBIE DOLL, RUPERT. I'LL SHOW YOU THE PROPER TECHNIQUE FOR THE SHARK ATTACK.

FIRST YOU SWIM SLOW, WIDE CIRCLES AROUND THE VICTIM WITH A CRAZED LOOK IN YOUR EYES.

SLOWLY TIGHTEN YOUR CIRCLES... THEN GO IN FOR THE KILL.

WOW, SO THAT'S HOW YOU EAT A SWIMMER.

THAT'S HOW YOU EAT A BARBIE.

IT CAME RIGHT OFF!

I HAD HIM BY HIS BATHING SUIT, AND THE NEXT THING YOU KNOW, HE WAS GONE!

YOU CAN'T GRAB A HAIRLESS BEACH APE BY THE BATHING SUIT, RUPERT, THEY'LL SLIP RIGHT OUT.

WOW. BUILT-IN UNDERWEAR.

LOOKS LIKE YOU SCARED HIM PRETTY GOOD.

THANKS FOR ALL THE SHARK LESSONS, UNCLE SHERMAN.

SOME DAY YOU'LL BE A BIG SHARK LIKE ME, RUPERT, AND YOU'LL BE MASTER OF YOUR OWN LAGOON.

SO LONG.

SEE YOU NEXT YEAR.

HE'S A GOOD KID. HE'LL GO FAR.

I'LL BET HE EATS A MEMBER OF CONGRESS ONE DAY.

SHERMAN'S LAGOON

BY J. TOOMEY

THAT'S A PRETTY HIGH TECH LOOKIN' CRAB THINGY, HAWTHORNE.

IT'S A CRAB PROBE.

WHEN THE MISSION IS TOO DANGEROUS FOR A REAL CRAB, YOU SEND ONE OF THESE BABIES.

TO PINCH WHERE NO CRAB HAS PINCHED BEFORE.

NOW LET'S HAVE A LOOK AT OUR MONITOR AND SEE WHAT'S UP THERE.

THERE'S A BEACH CHAIR... A COOLER... WE'RE GETTIN' WARM.

BINGO! THERE SHE IS! WHAT A BEAUTY... NOTHIN' BUT PINK!

SIGH

WHOA NELLY, THE SCREEN WENT BLACK.

CURSES! SHE ROLLED OVER ON ME!

SHERMAN, I HAVE BAD NEWS... REMEMBER THAT GUY WHO PERFORMED OUR WEDDING CEREMONY FOR TWENTY BUCKS?

YEAH. I JUST SAW HIS PICTURE IN THE PAPER. TURNS OUT HE'S A FRAUD.

THAT MEANS WE DIDN'T REALLY GET MARRIED SEVEN YEARS AGO.

I GUESS HE WASN'T THE REAL ELVIS PRESLEY EITHER. I'M AFRAID NOT.

MEGAN, ARE YOU TELLING ME WE HAVE TO GET MARRIED **AGAIN?** OUR FIRST WEDDING DIDN'T COUNT.

UGH... I DIDN'T EVEN ENJOY GETTING MARRIED THE FIRST TIME...

...NOW WE HAVE TO DO IT ALL OVER AGAIN.

HOW MANY DIVORCES IS IT GOING TO TAKE TO UNDO THIS THING? TWO DIVORCES, BUT ONLY ONE DEATH.

LOOK, I CAN STILL FIT INTO MY OLD WEDDING DRESS!

I'VE KEPT MY GIRLISH FIGURE ALL THESE YEARS. HOW DO I DO IT?

ALL SHE NEEDS IS ANOTHER DRESS JUST LIKE IT FOR THE BACK. I THINK SHE HEARD YOU.

Panel 1: DID I HEAR RIGHT? IS SHERMAN TAKING **DANCING** LESSONS?

Panel 2: YEP. HE SAID HE WANTED TO LOOK GOOD FOR THE WEDDING RECEPTION. / THAT ROMANTIC FOOL.

Panel 3: I CAN SEE US NOW... BRIDE AND GROOM OUT THERE ON THE DANCE FLOOR LIKE GINGER ROGERS AND FRED ASTAIRE.

Panel 4: *IT'S FUN TO STAY AT THE Y.M.C.A.* / IT'S NO USE. I CAN'T DANCE AND SPELL AT THE SAME TIME.

Panel 5: IT'S THE NIGHT BEFORE YOUR WEDDING. YOU KNOW WHAT **THAT** MEANS! / WHAT.

Panel 6: WE LET THE CHICKS DO THEIR LITTLE GIRLIE THING WHILE WE BOYS HIT THE TOWN.

Panel 7: I'LL TAKE YOU TO SOME OF MY OLD HANG OUTS. YOUR EYES ARE GOING TO POP OUT OF YOUR HEAD.

Panel 8: HAVE YOU EVER SEEN AN ALASKAN KING CRAB WITHOUT A SHELL? / IN A RESTAURANT.

Panel 9: DO YOU, SHERMAN, TAKE MEGAN TO BE YOUR LAWFULLY WEDDED WIFE?

Panel 10: ...TO HAVE AND TO HOLD FROM THIS DAY FORWARD?

Panel 11: ...FOR RICHER AND FOR POORER, IN SICKNESS AND IN HEALTH?

Panel 12: DO YOU SWEAR TO KEEP THE TOILET LID DOWN AND TAKE OUT THE TRASH? / THEY WROTE THEIR OWN VOWS.

SHERMAN'S LAGOON

BY J TOMEY

LOOK, HAWTHORNE, A FALLING STAR!

BRZZT!

BRZZT!

FWOOSH!

I'VE ALWAYS WONDERED ABOUT THOSE ANTENNAS.

DON'T ASK.

74

WE'RE LEAVING FOR OUR HONEY-MOON, FILLMORE. HOLD DOWN THE FORT.

HOW NICE. WHERE'RE YOU GOING?

WHERE ALL GREAT WHITE SHARKS GO ON THEIR HONEYMOON.

REALLY? I HAD NO IDEA THERE WAS SUCH A PLACE.

IT'S A LITTLE-KNOWN SCIENTIFIC FACT.

ENLIGHTEN ME. WHERE?

NIAGARA FALLS.

I'LL GET OUR HELMETS.

WE HAVE A DECISION TO MAKE, SHERMAN. THERE ARE THREE WAYS TO GET FROM THE PACIFIC TO THE ATLANTIC OCEAN...

TAHITI

ATLANTIC

BAJA

...WE COULD GO AROUND THE TIP OF SOUTH AMERICA, OR WE COULD SWIM THROUGH THE PANAMA CANAL...

...**OR** WE COULD ATTEMPT TO FIND THE FABLED NORTHWEST PASSAGE.

OF COURSE, THE GREATEST EXPLORERS OF WESTERN CIVILIZATION NEVER FOUND THE NORTHWEST PASSAGE.

I KNOW WHERE IT IS.

HOW'D WE END UP IN THE NEW YORK CITY SEWER SYSTEM?

IT'S THE SHORTEST ROUTE TO NIAGARA FALLS.

I THINK WE'RE LOST. LET'S ASK DIRECTIONS.

EXCUSE ME, COULD YOU TELL US HOW TO GET TO NIAGARA FALLS?

TAKE DA MAIN SEWAH LINE TO YONKERS, DEN HANG A LEFT.

HE WAS A NICE ENOUGH ALLIGATOR.

NEW YORK GETS A BAD RAP.

WE FINALLY MADE IT TO NIAGARA FALLS!

IT'S A LONG WAY DOWN.

LOOK WHAT'S COMING! HOT DIGGETY DOG!

THE LOCAL DELICACY.

FWUMP!

MAN-IN-A-BARREL.

LET'S OPEN 'ER UP.

WE'RE BACK.

THE HONEYMOON IS OVER, AS THEY SAY. WHAT COMES NEXT?

WE'RE NOW IN THE PHASE OF OUR MARRIAGE KNOWN AS "POST-NUPTIAL BLISS", WHICH VARIES IN DURATION, DEPENDING ON THE COUPLE.

THAT WAS FUN. WHAT'S NEXT?

WE COULD RENT A VIDEO.

HEY, HAWTHORNE, YOU GOT A PACKAGE.

HMPH. ABOUT TIME.

WHAT'RE THOSE THINGS?

ANTENNA EXTENDERS...

...THESE BABIES WILL ENHANCE MY SENSORY PERCEPTION, ALLOW ME TO COMMUNICATE TELEPATHICALLY, AND LET ME READ OTHER PEOPLES' MINDS.

CAN YOU GET E.S.P.N.?

THAT'S ANOTHER 6 BUCKS PER MONTH.

SHERMAN'S LAGOON
BY J. TOOMEY

SOMEBODY CALL A SAWFISH?

YEAH, I WANT YOU TO CUT THIS PIER DOWN.

THEN ALL THOSE PEOPLE WILL BE MINE...

THAT'S GOING TO RUN YOU 1,400 BUCKS.

1,400 BUCKS?

I'LL HAVE TO RENT SCAFFOLDING, PULL A PERMIT, AND PUT 4 SAWFISH ON IT FOR A WEEK.

FORGET IT!

SUIT YOURSELF.

1,400 BUCKS. HMPH!

THEY'LL SELL A SAW NOSE TO ANYBODY, WON'T THEY?

HOW HARD COULD THIS BE?

WHOA NELLY... THAT CHILI PEPPER IS SO STRONG IT WIPED OUT A THOUSAND VEGETARIAN PIRANHAS, AND THERE'S STILL HALF LEFT.

DARE YOU TO EAT IT.

SHERM?

(SNIFF) DID SOMEBODY FRY A FISH?

IT'S CRAB MOLTING SEASON AGAIN...THAT TIME OF YEAR WHEN ALL CRABS SHED THEIR SHELL AND STAY HIDDEN UNTIL THEY GET A NEW ONE.

I FEEL PRETTY I FEEL PRETTY LA LA LA LA LA LA

LA LA LAH! LA LA

NOT ALL CRABS STAY HIDDEN.

OURS IS A LITTLE LAID BACK ABOUT THE NUDITY THING.

A NAKED HERMIT CRAB. THAT COULD MEAN ONLY ONE THING.

THE SUMMER FASHIONS ARE OUT AND I NEED A NEW SHELL.

BUT THERE ARE TOO MANY CHOICES THIS YEAR...

ARMANI, LAUREN, HILFIGER...

...BUDWEISER.

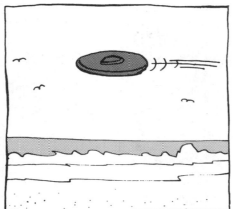

WHAT HAPPENED TO YOU, FAT BOY? YOU'RE ALL COVERED WITH SPOTS!

REMEMBER THAT TOURIST I ATE YESTERDAY?

YEAH.

TURNED OUT SHE WAS A RED HEAD. I'M ALLERGIC TO RED HEADS.

I THOUGHT SHE WAS WEARING A WIG.

SHE HAD RED HAIR UNDER HER RED WIG.

WOMEN! DON'T TRY TO FIGURE THEM OUT! JES LEAVE 'EM BE!

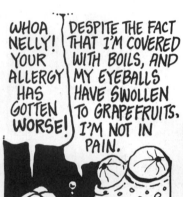

WHOA NELLY! YOUR ALLERGY HAS GOTTEN WORSE!

DESPITE THE FACT THAT I'M COVERED WITH BOILS, AND MY EYEBALLS HAVE SWOLLEN TO GRAPEFRUITS, I'M NOT IN PAIN.

WELL, IT HURTS ME TO LOOK AT YOU!

OW!

AND IF I'M GOING TO BE IN PAIN, SO ARE YOU!

ANYTHING I CAN DO TO MAKE THIS EASIER FOR YOU.

YOU DON'T LOOK HEALTHY.

I'M HAVING A SLIGHT ALLERGIC REACTION TO SOMETHING I ATE.

YOU COULD USE A GOOD BLOOD SUCKING. ONLY 20 BUCKS.

GET AWAY FROM ME, YOU LEECH!

DON'T INSULT ME! WOULD A LEECH CHARGE TO SUCK YOUR BLOOD?

I GUESS NOT.

I'M A VASCULAR CONSULTANT.

WELL, SHOOT... 20 BUCKS SOUNDS LIKE A DEAL.

SHERMAN'S LAGOON

BY J. TOOMEY

YOU KNOW, HAWTHORNE, SOMETIMES IT'S TOUGH BEING A SHARK...

... MASTER OF THE REEF, KING OF THE PREDATORS...

IT'S NOT EASY BEING KING. EVERYONE LOOKS UP TO YOU.

ARGH!

GROSS! A JELLYFISH! GET IT AWAY FROM ME!

ARGH! IT'S FOLLOWING ME! GET AWAY! GET AWAY!

AFTER A BRIEF POWER STRUGGLE, I'M BACK ON THE THRONE. UNTIL THE NEXT JELLYFISH.

SEAWEED? THAT'S ALL YOU WANT FOR DINNER? ARE YOU SOME KIND OF FISH-MAN?

UH OH... I THINK SHE'S ON TO ME. ACT COOL.

YOUR DINNER, MA'AM.

THANK YOU.

ARGH!

WHAT IS IT?

I THINK I KNOW YOUR LOBSTER.

I BEG YOUR PARDON?

I HAD A WONDERFUL TIME, VERONICA.

THANKS FOR THE NICE DINNER, FILLMORE.

I'LL CALL YOU SOME TIME

I'M OUT OF TOWN A LOT.

I GUESS THIS IS WHERE WE PART WAYS FOR THE EVENING.

I'D KISS YOU, BUT MY NOSE IS TOO HUGE.

SAVED BY A NOSE.

WE'VE WANDERED PRETTY FAR FROM HOME, ERNEST.

JUST A LITTLE FARTHER. I SEE SOMETHING OVER THERE.

WHOA NELLY.

YOU KNOW WHAT I THINK WE'VE FOUND, SHERM? THE LOST CITY OF ATLANTIS!

BUT, HOW DO WE KNOW THIS IS THE REAL LOST CITY OF ATLANTIS?

LOOK. THE LOST CITY OF ATLANTIS YELLOW PAGES.

WELL, KISS MY GRITS!

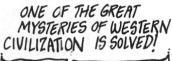

93

I GUESS IF WE'RE GOING TO VISIT THE LOST CITY OF ATLANTIS, WE SHOULD PICK UP A SOUVENIR.

HOW ABOUT THIS MINI IONIC COLUMN?

BORE ME.

HOW ABOUT THIS LIQUID-FILLED X-RATED PAPER WEIGHT

BUT, IT'S GOT NOTHING TO DO WITH ATLANTIS.

LOOK WHAT HAPPENS WHEN YOU TILT IT.

GROSS. LET'S GET IT.

WE'VE JUST RETURNED FROM THE LOST CITY OF ATLANTIS!

WE FOUND IT!

HMPH. WELL, I GUESS SOMEBODY WAS BOUND TO FIND IT SOONER OR LATER.

YOU DON'T IMPRESS EASILY, DO YOU?

IT'S JUST AN OLD SUNKEN CITY.

WE BROUGHT BACK AN X-RATED PAPER WEIGHT.

OOH COOL!

HEY, HAWTHORNE, WHAT THE HECK DO YOU THINK THESE THINGS ARE?

HMPH. THEY'VE GOT FINS... MAYBE THEY'RE SOME KIND OF WEIRD FISH. HELLO? HELLO?

COME TO THINK OF IT, THEY LOOK LIKE BOMBS.

WELL, THEY DON'T TASTE LIKE FISH.

YOU ATE ONE?

Panel 1: WELCOME BACK TO KAPUPU ISLAND, THORNTON. / OOH! IS THAT FOR ME?

Panel 2: YEP. I FIXED YOU A TROPICAL DRINK. IT'S CALLED A "SMOOTHIE." / SCHWEET. WHAT'S INNIT?

Panel 3: IT'S GOT ICE—POLAR BEARS LOVE ICE—, AND MANGOS, AND PAPAYA...

Panel 4: IS THAT AN EYEBALL? / I BLENDED A HERRING IN THERE FOR YOU.

Panel 5: NEW BATHING SUIT? / YEP. COULDN'T FIT INTO LAST YEAR'S SUIT. I'VE PICKED UP A LITTLE BABY FAT.

Panel 6: OH WELL... NEEDED A NEW ONE ANYWAY.

Panel 7: NOW FOR THE **REAL** TEST...

Panel 8: CAN I FIT IN LAST YEAR'S BEACH CHAIR? / LOOKS LIKE YOU NEED A NEW ONE OF THOSE, TOO.

Panel 9: DID YOU **REALLY** JUST ARRIVE FROM THE NORTH POLE? / YEP.

Panel 10: WOULD YOU HAPPEN TO KNOW THE FAMOUS SANTA CLAUS? / I'M PRETTY TIGHT WITH ONE OF THE ELVES.

Panel 12: HERE'S $10,000 IN SMALL BILLS. GET ME SOME BEENIE BABIES. / I'LL SEE WHAT I CAN DO.

ANOTHER DAY IN PARADISE. I THINK I'LL DIG MY TOES INTO THE WARM SAND AND READ A TOM CLANCY NOVEL.

BLEETLE BLEEP BLEETLE BLEEP BLEETLE BLEEP

HELLO? YEAH... THEY WANT TO DO ANOTHER COKE COMMERCIAL? ... WHEN? ... OKAY... BYE.

ALL MY CLIENTS THINK I'M STILL AT THE NORTH POLE.

THE MIRACLE OF CALL FORWARDING.

SHERMAN THE SHARK!

THORNTON THE POLAR BEAR!

HOW'S THE FEROCIOUS CARNIVORE BUSINESS TREATING YOU?

NOT BAD. I JUST FINISHED DOING A NATURE DOCUMENTARY. HOW 'BOUT YOU?

OH, YOU KNOW... A LITTLE OF THIS, A LITTLE OF THAT...

I SPENT TWO MONTHS AS A MASCOT FOR A HOCKEY TEAM IN CANADA.

IS THERE ANY MONEY IN THAT?

LOOKS LIKE AN INVITATION FOR YOU, HAWTHORNE.

HMPH... IT'S THE ANNUAL CHRISTMAS ISLAND CRAB STAMPEDE.

THE WHAT?

CRABS COME FROM ALL OVER AND DESCEND ON CHRISTMAS ISLAND. HUMANS EVACUATE, CATTLE FLEE.

I'M NOT SURE I WANT TO ATTEND AFTER LAST YEAR'S FIASCO.

WE WALKED STRAIGHT INTO THE CHRISTMAS ISLAND SEAFOOD FESTIVAL.

BAD TIMING.

SHERMAN'S LAGOON

BY TOOMEY

You're blocking the entrance to my crab hole, fat boy! That's not allowed! *MPH!*

Says who?

It's the law of the sea!

Law of the sea... baloney.

You don't believe me? I'll get a sea lawyer!

HMPH!

Section 23, paragraph 4 of the law of the sea: "Sharks shall grant crabs rights of egress on aforementioned crab's crab hole."

HMPH! Told you!

That'll be $400.

$400!

WHOA!

What's it say in there about eating lawyers?

What lawyer?

SHERMAN'S LAGOON

BY J.P. TOOMEY

I THINK I'VE GOT SOMETHING.

YEP. I'VE DEFINITELY GOT SOMETHING.

REEL HIM IN SLOW.

LET HIM REEL YOU IN SLOW.

DO YOU SEE HIM?

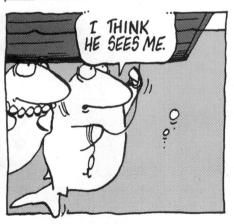

I THINK HE SEES ME.

A LITTLE CLOSER.

I'LL GET HIM WITH THE NET.

HEY, YOU IN THERE! THAT'S MY CRAB HOLE AND I DEMAND THAT YOU VACATE IMMEDIATELY!

IF YOU **DON'T** COME OUT, THEN I HAVE NO CHOICE BUT TO LEAVE YOU TO THE MERCY OF A FEROCIOUS SHARK WHO ENJOYS EATING CREEPS LIKE YOU FOR BREAKFAST!

ARGH!

GO FIND YOUR WIFE.

YO, MEGAN!

LOOKS LIKE WE'RE GOING TO BE ROOM MATES, AT LEAST UNTIL THAT BEAST MOVES OUT OF MY CRAB HOLE.

I HAVE TO WARN YOU, SOMETIMES I TALK IN MY SLEEP.

SOMETIMES I EAT IN MY SLEEP.

I'M OUTTA HERE.

HAWTHORNE? IS THAT YOU?

ZZZZZ...
HMPH!

IS IT MORNING ALREADY?

YES... WHY AREN'T YOU WAKING UP IN YOUR OWN CRAB HOLE?

I'VE BEEN FORCED OUT BY SOME NASTY CRITTER.

CAN YOU SPARE $3.50 FOR A CAPPUCCINO?

WHEN YOU GO HOMELESS, YOU GO IN STYLE.

WHY DON'T YOU STAY AT MY PLACE UNTIL YOU CAN MOVE BACK INTO YOUR CRAB HOLE?

A GENEROUS OFFER I CAN'T REFUSE.

YOU CAN LEARN HOW TO CHANGE A DIAPER WHILE YOU'RE HERE.

OH DANDY.

LOOKS LIKE IT'S TIME FOR YOUR FIRST LESSON.

I CAN'T WAIT.

OH, THAT'S A GOOD ONE.

WHAT'S A BAD ONE LOOK LIKE?

THAT BEAST FINALLY MOVED OUT OF MY CRAB HOLE!

IT'LL NEVER BE THE SAME! THE PLACE IS A SHAMBLES... A **SHAMBLES** I TELL YOU!

HE PUT SOME FOO-FOO IRISH CREAM COFFEE BEANS IN MY ESPRESSO MACHINE!

THE BARBARIAN.

SNIFF SNIFF

WHAT ON EARTH ARE YOU DOING?

TESTING THE NOSE UNIT. SHARKS DEPEND ON THEIR RAZOR-SHARP SENSE OF SMELL.

(SNIFF) RIGHT NOSTRIL'S CLEAR, BUT NOW THE LEFT ONE'S CLOGGED.

I NEED TO BORROW YOUR TOOTHBRUSH AGAIN.

WHEN DID YOU USE MY TOOTHBRUSH?

THE BEACH CLEAN UP IS GOING GREAT. WE'VE COLLECTED A TON OF GARBAGE.

HEY, GUYS, LOOK WHAT **I** FOUND!

YOU DON'T FIND A BARREL OF THIS STUFF EVERY DAY... TASTES KINDA STALE, THOUGH.

YOU **ATE** SOME OF IT?

ISN'T THIS THE INTERNATIONAL SYMBOL FOR PIE FILLING?

NOPE. RADIOACTIVE WASTE.

IT'S RADIOACTIVE ALL RIGHT. THAT MEANS WE'VE ALL BEEN CONTAMINATED.

OH WELL, WHAT'S A LITTLE RADIOACTIVITY AMONG FRIENDS?

LOOK AT THE BRIGHT SIDE...

WE'RE NO LONGER ELIGIBLE TO BECOME SUSHI.

WELL, THAT'S ONE LESS WORRY.

WHERE DO YOU THINK THE PIPE LEADS?

FAR AWAY FROM HERE. THAT'S ALL THAT MATTERS.

I'M NOT SURE THIS IS A RESPONSIBLE WAY TO DISPOSE OF RADIOACTIVE WASTE.

THERE'S NO DISPOSING OF IT. YOU JUST KEEP MOVING IT AROUND.

READY TO START THE PUMP?

READY.

OKAY, WHO FILLED THE BATH TUB WITH LIME JELLO?

I DIDN'T DO IT.

LOOK AT THIS LITTLE CLAM, MEGAN.

HE'S GOT A LITTLE CLAM MOTHER AND A LITTLE CLAM FATHER...

HE'S GOT A LITTLE CLAM PERSONALITY... HE DREAMS CLAM DREAMS... HAS CLAM ASPIRATIONS...

...AND YOU CAN GET A WHOLE BUCKET OF THEM FOR A DOLLAR.

PASS THE COCKTAIL SAUCE.

THAT'S A MIGHTY SMALL FENCE.

IT'S AN OYSTER RANCH.

AN OYSTER RANCH?

PEARLS ARE BIG MONEY. THIS HERD OF OYSTERS IS GOING TO MAKE ME RICH.

HYAH! WHOA! HYAH!

CUTE LITTLE CRITTERS.

THAT ONE'S A BULL. GIVE HIM A WIDE BERTH.

HOW'S LIFE ON THE OYSTER RANCH, SHERM?

DANDY. WE SHOULD HAVE A FINE CROP OF PEARLS THIS YEAR.

THE HERD'S A LITTLE FEISTY. IT'S BRANDING DAY.

PSSSSSSSSS

WENT A LITTLE HARD ON THAT ONE.

CARE FOR AN APPETIZER?

SHERMAN'S LAGOON

BY J.P. TOOMEY

WHOA NELLY! A SEA SNAKE!

MUNCH MUNCH MUNCH MUNCH

STAY AWAY FROM THE ONES WITH THE STRIPES...

MUNCH GULP

...THEY'RE THE BAD ONES. INSTANT DEATH. BYE BYE.

ARGH!

DON'T BITE ME! I'LL DO ANYTHING YOU ASK, JUST DON'T BITE ME!

YOU'RE A LITTLE SPEED BOAT. LET'S HEAR YOUR MOTOR.

PUTT PUTT PUTTER PUTT PUTTER PUTT PUTT.

NOW YOU'RE A PIECE OF BACON. FRY LIKE BACON.

PSSSSS SSSS POPSS POP SSS SSSS

I'M HOME.

WHAT'S WRONG WITH THAT SHARK?

SHERMAN'S LAGOON

BY J.TOOMEY

JUST ONCE WHY CAN'T WE GO TO A **NORMAL** RESTAURANT, MEGAN?

PERFORMANCE FOOD IS ALL THE RAGE, SHERMAN. JUST GIVE IT A TRY.

VOILA, YOUR APPETIZER... ZEE SHAKESPEARIAN SHRIMP.

THANK YOU.

TO BE OR NOT TO BE? THAT IS THE QUESTION.

TIS A FAIR QUESTION. BUT FIRST, A SWORD FIGHT.

CLINK CLINK **CLANK** CLINK CLINK

I, FOR ONE, WOULD RATHER BE THAN **NOT** BE.

ME TOO.

ME THREE.

'TIS TIME TO BE GONE.

ALACK AND ANON, AND SO ON, AND SO ON.

ISN'T SOMEBODY SUPPOSED TO DIE AT THE END?

OH, WAITER...

AS YOUR MANAGER, I'D SAY YOUR CONCERT WAS AN UNQUALIFIED SUCCESS. WHALES LOVE YOU, MAN. YOU'RE A STAR!

WHAT'S IT FEEL LIKE TO BE LOVED BY WHALES?

UNGH.

YOU'RE STARTING TO TALK LIKE A ROCK STAR ALREADY... HERE'S A BONUS.

IF YOU DON'T STOP SMASHING YOUR GUITAR AFTER EVERY CONCERT, YOU'LL NEVER MAKE ANY MONEY AT THIS.

UNGH.

GOOD NEWS, SHERMAN, WE'VE GONE PLATINUM!

WHAT'S **THAT** MEAN?

THAT MEANS YOU'RE NOW LIKE ALL OTHER ROCK STARS, THANKS TO MY SHREWD MANAGEMENT.

YAHOO!

WE'VE GONE PLATINUM!

VISA <u>AND</u> AMERICAN EXPRESS.

YOU ARE THE HOTTEST ROCK STAR IN THE OCEAN RIGHT NOW, AND THIS CONCERT IS GOING TO PROVE IT.

NOW TAKE THAT STAGE AND SING THOSE WHALE SONGS! MAKE THOSE WHALES SWOON! THEY LOVE YOU! GO!

ARGH!

WHOP!

WHAT WAS THAT?

A GARTER BELT. SHAKE IT OFF, CHAMP.

OATMEAL? THATS WHAT THE LEGENDARY LOCH NESS MONSTER EATS FOR BREAKFAST?

AYE.

WHAT KIND OF MONSTER EATS OATMEAL FOR BREAKFAST? HEE HEE HEE!

WE SHARKS LIKE THE TASTE OF FLESH AND BLOOD... EVEN IN THE MORNING.

WHAT'S IN **YOUR** CEREAL BOWL?

GRAVY TRAIN.

YOU'RE LEAVING US ALREADY, NESSIE?

AYE. I MUST BE GETTIN' BACK TO LOCH NESS.

YA SEE, LAD, SCOTLAND MAY BE COLD AND WINDY AND WET, BUT IT'S HOME TO ME.

I WISH I COULD STAY IN THE SOUTH PACIFIC FOREVER. 'TIS PARADISE IT IS.

WHEN THEY'RE NOT TESTING NUCLEAR BOMBS.

AYE. IT'S ALWAYS SOMETHIN'.

IS THAT SINGING COMING FROM BOB THE BOTTOM DWELLER?

I BELIEVE IT IS.

SOUNDS LIKE... ...OPERA.

COULD IT BE THAT THIS DISGUSTING LITTLE CREATURE IS IN FACT A MUSICAL VIRTUOSO AND WE DIDN'T KNOW IT?

HICCUP BURP!

NOW HE'S SINGING SALSA.

HE SWALLOWED A RADIO.

SHERMAN'S LAGOON

BY TOOMEY

YOU'VE GOT JUNK MAIL!

ANOTHER COLD DAY AND NOBODY'S ON THE BEACH.

IT'S BEEN A WHOLE WEEK. WE'LL HAVE TO RESORT TO SEAFOOD SOON.

GOOD NEWS. PRETTY SOON YOU'LL HAVE ALL THE HAIRLESS BEACH APES THAT YOU CAN EAT.

I SENT E-MAILS TO 100,000 PEOPLE PROMISING THEM FREE MONEY IF THEY SWIM IN OUR LAGOON.

SURELY YOU DON'T THINK ANYBODY'S GOING TO FALL FOR **THAT**, DO YOU?

MEGAN, LOOK! UP ON THE BEACH!

DID Y'ALL GET THAT E-MAIL ABOUT FREE MONEY?

YEAH.

I THOUGHT I WAS THE ONLY ONE WHO GOT THAT E-MAIL.

HMMM... THIS WHOLE INTERNET THING IS INTRIGUING.

I DON'T EAT STUPID PEOPLE.

YEAH, WE HAVE OUR STANDARDS.